Eight Town

WRITTEN BY NANCY LOEWEN • ILLUSTRATED BY RONNIE ROONEY

The Child's World®

Published by The Child's World®
1980 Lookout Drive • Mankato, MN 56003-1705
800-599-READ • www.childsworld.com

ACKNOWLEDGMENTS
The Child's World®: Mary Berendes, Publishing Director
The Design Lab: Design and production
Red Line Editorial: Editorial direction

LIBRARY OF CONGRESS CATALOGING-IN-PUBLICATION DATA
Loewen, Nancy, 1964–
  Eight town / written by Nancy Loewen ;
illustrated by Ronnie Rooney.
    p. cm.
  ISBN 978-1-60253-497-1 (lib. bd. : alk. paper)
  1. Eight (The number)—Juvenile literature. 2. Number concept—
Juvenile literature. I. Rooney, Ronnie, ill. II. Title. III. Title: 8 town.
  QA141.3.L643 2010
  513.2—dc22   2010007542

Printed in the United States of America in Mankato, Minnesota.
July 2010
F11538

About the Author

Nancy Loewen has published
almost 100 books for children.
She lives in Prior Lake, Minnesota,
with 1 husband, 2 kids, 2 cats, 1 dog,
and 1 guinea pig. Altogether that's
16 eyes, 8 noses, 8 mouths, 16 ears, and
150 fingers, toes, and claws.

About the Illustrator

Ronnie Rooney was born and raised
in Massachusetts. She attended the
University of Massachusetts at
Amherst for her undergraduate study
and Savannah College of Art and Design
for her MFA in illustration. Ronnie has
illustrated numerous books for children.
She hopes to pass this love of art on to her daughter.

8

eight

Every **8** in **Eight** Town loves the number **8**.

All the buildings in **Eight** Town have **eight** floors.

Even the houses!

Eight Town has a lot of stop signs. **8**s just love things with **eight** sides. But it takes a long time to get to school in the morning!

At school, young **8**s love art class the best. Crayons come in boxes of **eight**. The **8**s use all **eight** colors at once.

In gym class, bouncy **8**s jump rope and turn somersaults with ease.

But they always have trouble on the balance beam.

After school, Eddie **8** goes to the aquarium with his mom. They love to see the octopus and its **eight** arms.

Eddie invites **eight** friends over for dinner.

Good thing Eddie's dad always cooks **eight** things.

Eddie and his friends play Crazy **Eights** after dinner. Ellie **8** wins **eight** times in a row!

But, everyone in **Eight** Town is gr-*eight*!

What Makes Eight?

Here are eight pieces of candy.
Cover one with your hand.
How many are left?

Cover three candies with your hand.
How many are left?

Now, cover four candies.
What number goes with 4 to make 8?

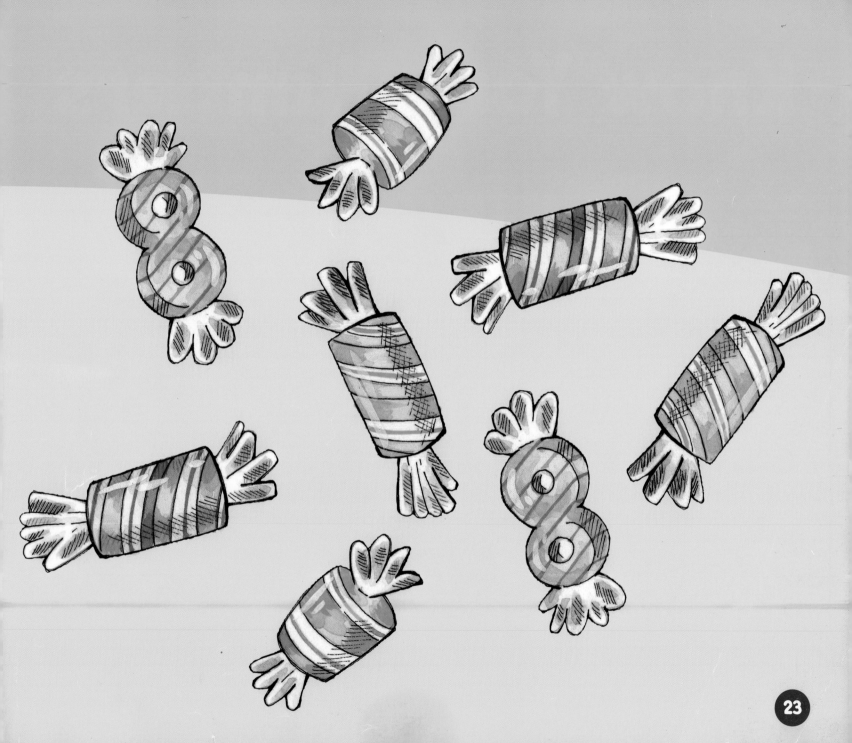

Know Your Numbers

Hola, 8!

In Spanish, the number "eight" is ocho. Say it: *OH-choh*.

Eight Riddle

Here is one popular riddle from Eight Town. Why is 6 afraid of 7? Because 7 "ate" 9!

Scary Spiders?

The 8s in Eight Town aren't afraid of spiders. Can you guess why? Spiders have eight legs!

The Eight Ball

In the game of pool, the eight ball is very important. Players must hit all of their other balls into the pockets before hitting the eight ball. But whoever hits the eight ball in at the end of the game wins!

Find Eight

Can you find all the things that come in eights in this book? How many groups of eight are there?